D1397237

The Blue Angel
Ornament

To my granddaughters
Sarah, Hilary, Katrina

THE BLUE ANGEL ORNAMENT

RICHARD H. SCHNEIDER

ILLUSTRATED BY

FLORENCE S. DAVIS

Abingdon Press
Nashville

THE BLUE ANGEL ORNAMENT

Copyright © 2000 by Abingdon Press

Library of Congress Cataloging-in-Publication Data

Schneider, Richard H., 1922-
   The blue angel ornament / Richard H. Schneider ; illustrated by Florence S. Davis.
     p. cm.
   Summary: Although it had been so happy to be a family's Christmas tree, a fir tree is afraid when it learns that it will be burned now that the holiday is over--until a selfless angel ornament promises to stay with the tree.
   ISBN 0-687-08181-5 (alk. paper)
   [1. Christmas trees--Fiction. 2. Christmas--Fiction. 3. Loyalty--Fiction. 4. Christian life--Fiction.] I. Davis, Florence S., ill. II. Title.

PZ7.S36425 B1 2000
[E]--dc21
                                            99-088389

00 01 02 03 04 05 06 07 08 09—10 9 8 7 6 5 4 3 2 1

PRINTED IN HONG KONG

Everyone in town wondered about the rare and beautiful violets growing in the park that spring. They couldn't remember seeing any of that particular color and size ever before. Moreover, they were growing in a spot that, despite the diligent work of the gardeners, had remained bare of grass and flowers as long as anyone could remember.

It all began after Christmas at the Johnsons' house when it was time to take down the tree. A bit dry and scruffy, with no gifts below, the fir tree huddled forlornly in the living room.

"Just when are you going to take down that tree, Dad?" called out a woman's voice.

"This afternoon, Mother, like I promised," came the man's reply from the basement.

The tree shivered. "Now what?" he wondered aloud.

"Oh," sighed a golden ball ornament near the peak, "you'll be thrown out and burned in a few days." The ornament twirled back to the excited chatter of the other decorations that had hung on the fir's branches these past weeks. Once they had twisted and sparkled in the rainbow-glow of tree lights. Now the electric cord was unplugged, and the light bulbs hung cold and dim.

But the ornaments were wide awake, discussing their future. "Oooaah," yawned a scarlet glass bird. "I'll be so glad to snuggle back into my tissue nest and sleep till next year."

"Yes, but wasn't my performance wonderful this year?" preened the lavender ballerina, who always thought she contributed most to the display.

"*We* were wonderful," chimed the shiny silver bell. Then he added, "but I do hope we'll be given a better tree next time. The good branches this year were so low, I didn't show off as well as I could."

The fir tree winced, but said nothing. His little heart chilled with loneliness and fear of the unknown future.

From the day he was a seedling growing with his brothers and sisters in the Christmas-tree forest up north, he had enjoyed being with others. As the fir sprigs grew, basking in the summer sun, drinking in the rain, bracing against the winter winds, they were happy. They had talked excitedly above the wind humming through their branches.

When the little fir heard that he was being grown for a Christmas tree, his root-toes curled with delight. Of all the trees, none loved the company of others as much as he. The very thought of being with so many people warmed his heart as he listened to talk of what lay ahead.

And so it happened, late that fall. He had no fear when he heard the sound of the ax in the forest. When his turn came, he toppled with joy for he knew he would soon be a part of the wonderful festival of Christmas.

Stacked with other trees on a truck, he was taken into the city. Then came long days of waiting in the tree lot until one afternoon a strong hand hefted his trunk and a man said, "I'll take this one."

All that the little fir tree had heard of the wonderful life of Christmas trees came true, more than he had ever imagined. He was decorated with many colored lights and fabulous ornaments. Laughing children played under his branches, and grownups admired his handsome shape . . . until now, the last few days since Christmas Day, when no one seemed interested in him anymore.

The tree shivered; he missed the warmth of the lights. But more than that, he was frightened. His needles cringed as he remembered the words of the golden ball ornament: "You'll be taken out and burned."

No one had ever mentioned this. The little tree stifled a sob.

And then he heard a small voice deep within his branches, "Don't worry. It isn't as bad as all that."

The tree looked down to the tinkly voice. It came from an ornament he had not noticed before, a little blue angel with silver wings and spun-gold hair.

"I know how you feel," she said. "But that's the way life is. Nothing ever remains the same. We come and we go. Even we ornaments can't expect to stay here very long. Each year two or three of us are broken, and we're swept away with the trash. I've been lucky so far."

Still the little tree shuddered. "But I'm so frightened to be alone," he whispered, a tear oozing from his trunk.

The little angel was silent. Her tinsel heart was touched. She had been looking forward to a warm bed of tissue and a pleasant summer's sleep in the attic with dreams of another Christmas to come. She had been a special ornament, this one, to survive so many years.

But she saw the fir tree's tear slide down his trembling trunk, and felt his sad loneliness. Then—perhaps it was because she had listened to the old, old story on so many Christmas Eves when the family gathered before the fire and the father read from a book about how God had given his son, Jesus, to come to earth and give his life for others . . .

O r perhaps, she . . . Who knows why hearts suddenly open?

But the little blue angel piped in sudden bravado, "Don't worry, friend. I'll stay with you."

"Stay with me?" echoed the fir tree. "Can you do that?"

"Oh, sure," promised the angel. "I know what to do. I'll just twist out of sight when the man removes the other decorations. He can't see too well now, anyway."

And that's how it happened. When the man took down the tree, he missed one ornament, a little blue angel that squeezed between two bushy branches and hung there with all her might as he carried the fir tree out of the house.

The two clung together in the deep snow in the backyard. The ornament was amazed at this new world of cold fresh air. She felt vibrant and alive with the caress of the wind and blinked in awe at the star-studded sky above. "And I thought I had seen lights!" she tinkled breathlessly.

Through the days and nights, the two carried on the long conversation of good friends when time slips by unnoticed. The fir tree revealed the secrets of nature to his angel-friend. And not only did the blue angel learn about real birds instead of glass ones, but visited with them when they fluttered into the fir branches to rest. She learned how they flew and the mysterious way God guided them on their long journeys.

She learned other wonderful things from the fir tree: why the stars twinkled more on cold nights, how to understand the hymns sung by the wind, and how all growing things—like people and animals, trees and flowers—were created by a wonderful, magnificent God.

The angel gave of her knowledge too, and the fir learned about things made by humankind—how the ornament, once a thimble-full of sand, was melted into glass and blown into sparkling form with glistening wings. And, best of all, he learned of Christmases past and of other trees before his time. The fir tree and the little blue angel were supremely happy together.

Then on a cold black night—the twelfth night of Christmas—the time came. A bright glow filled the sky. It was time for the town's Christmas tree burning. The tree and the little blue angel didn't talk much, but quietly waited unafraid.

Soon the fir tree was lifted to the top of an automobile. It was a short trip to the bonfire. When the tree saw the scene, he gripped the angel tightly. Before him were dozens of trees, just like him, ablaze in the hot bright light, crackling into a torrent of sparks that flew into the night.

A man in a red helmet took the fir tree from Mr. Johnson's hand and walked swiftly toward the blaze. As he did, a little boy saw the glint of blue within the fir's branches and shouted, "Look, there's an ornament in that tree!"

When the gloved hand reached for her, the blue ornament hesitated. She knew if she allowed herself to be rescued, she would probably spend many more happy Christmases in a warm home.

But she had made a promise to her friend, and she wiggled deeper into his branches so she couldn't be seen. In an instant, the fir tree and his passenger were part of the flame. Everyone noticed that this one tree blazed so much brighter, almost as if in joyful celebration.

Later, when there was nothing left but a pile of cooling ashes, the gardeners came with shovels and wheelbarrows. One particular pile of ashes had a strange blue tinge. A gardener scooped up that pile and scattered the ashes on a bare spot of earth.

That spring, the bare spot blossomed into an amazing display of violets. People from far and wide came to see them. They were unlike any violet that had ever bloomed before. The flowers were a beautiful azure blue, the color of the sky on a fresh spring morning.

Looking at them made everyone's heart glow, for each blue flower was an expression of God's love and a promise kept by the little blue angel.